Gary Stevenson

The Tides & Tales Of A True Master In The Arduous Game Of Trading

Copyright© 2024 by Steve Hary

All rights reserved. No part of this book may be reproduced or transmitted in any form or by any means, electronic or mechanical, including photocopying, recording, or by any information storage and retrieval system, without written permission from the publisher, except for the inclusion of brief quotations in a review or scholarly journal.

DEDICATION

To God almighty who made this possible and to the readers who dedicate their time for knowledge's sake.

This short read is for you.

Table of contents

CHAPTER 1: INTRODUCTION — 5
CHAPTER 2: EARLY LIFE — 7
CHAPTER 3: GARY STEVENSON'S SPEECH ABOUT HIS CAREER LIFE — 10
CHAPTER 4: CAREER — 17
CHAPTER 5: TRADING JOURNEY — 22
CHAPTER 6: GARY'S TRADING TRICKS — 26
CHAPTER 7: CONCLUSION — 42

CHAPTER 1: INTRODUCTION

(Who Is Gary Stevenson?)

Gary Stevenson is a UK-based economist trader known on YouTube as GarysEcononics.

He is a former interest rate trader and equality campaigner based in London and Tokyo.

Gary is known for becoming Citi Bank's most profitable trader in 2011 by predicting there would be an increase in economic inequality.

He campaigns on the issue of wealth inequality. Through his organization, Gary's Economics, he helps make the opaque world of finance and wealth comprehensible, in plain language, and he explains how inequality becomes entrenched and perpetuated.

He is also focused on teaching people about real-world economics, and inequality economics.

CHAPTER 2: EARLY LIFE

Gary Stevenson hails from Aelfred in East London.

He grew up with his brother, (who is now a computer programmer) and a sister (who is a poet) in a cramped two-bed terrace backing onto a railway line in Ilford, east London,

Gary Stevenson was born in 1987.

Right from birth, he always wanted to make a lot of money. *"I was a clever, poor, ambitious kid, who just*

didn't want to be poor anymore," he told the news.

Stevenson's father was a Post Office worker in Ilford. As a child, Stevenson worked as a paperboy, he went to Ilford County High School, from which he was later expelled at the age of 16 due to a "drug-related" transgression.[3]

In the year 2005, Gary Stevenson enrolled in the London School of Economics and studied Maths and economics.

Gary, grew up in poverty in England, worked for Citibank in Tokyo and London after winning a position there through a game card and in 2011 became the bank's most profitable trader globally by correctly predicting that the after-effects of the 2008 financial crisis would lead to a long term stagnation in interest rates and a rapid rise in asset values. He retired from the City in 2014 aged just 27, as a multimillionaire, to study economics and inequality at Oxford University. He is currently working on economic models of inequality, wages and asset prices.

He has BSc in Maths and economics, London School of Economics. MPhil in economics, Oxford.

CHAPTER 3: GARY STEVENSON'S SPEECH ABOUT HIS CAREER LIFE

Gary Stevenson's Establishment

In one of his videos on his YouTube page; Garyseconomics. Gary talked about his life and how he was able to become a millionaire in 2010 at 23 years old.

"My name is Gary Stevenson, I grew up in east London from a poor family, in quite a poor area

Back in 2008, when I was 21, I got a job working for Citibank in Canary Whart.

Now my job was to bet on whether interest rates would go up or down. Interest rates go up when the economy is strong and down when the economy is weak.

So basically my job was to bet on the strength of the global economy. Now when I started to work in 2008, there was a global financial crisis and all the rates, in the whole world Came down to zero. So very quickly, my job was to bet on when the rates would recover. which is basically a bet on when the global economy will recover.

Now the issue of this is super interesting, right?

In 2008 governments and central banks, printed a huge amount of money and pushed it into the economy. That meant that stock prices bounced super quickly and economists and traders predicted that the global economy would recover quickly as well.

So in 2008, they predicted a rapid recovery in 2009. In 2009, when that recovery didn't happen, they pushed the prediction back to 2010. In 2010, it got pushed back to 2011. In 2011, it got pushed back to 2012. In 2012, it was 2013, and on and on, and back last year in 2020, they were still predicting a recovery for later that year which is 2022.

And here we are in 2021 with global interest rates just as the global economy is still at its lowest emergency.

Now, before I started working in the city, I studied Economics And I became fascinated by understanding, why are our predictions always wrong. Why do we always predict that the economy is going to recover, when it doesn't recover? When is the economy going to recover? Will it ever recover? when it doesn't recover. And underlying those questions is one big question. Why aren't people spending more money? Now in 2008 when this huge wave of new money got pushed into the economy, economists thought people were going to spend this money and that was going to cause a massive economic boom. When that didn't happen, economists didn't understand why.

But for me, having grown up in a place like East London, around here. I felt I could understand why. Now if you print a huge amount of money. it's important where that money goes. People like my family, People like the people I grew up with, people like the people around here , who would have spent that money, if they got it, weren't getting it.

Instead, the money were going to people like, the people I was working with in the city or even the super-rich people, whose money we were moving.

Now when these people get money they don't spend it, They use it to buy assets like stocks and property. They use it to buy assets like stocks and property. That means that it doesn't boost the economy. All it does is push up stock and house prices. Now when house prices go up, that doesn't help ordinary people in fact, it makes it harder for ordinary people to buy houses. That means if we print money, but it only goes to the rich, it doesn't make the economy better, in fact, it makes the economy worse.

Now I can see that if we don't fix inequality, the global economy is not going to recover.

Since economists and politicians weren't doing anything about it I could tell that the economy wasn't going to get better any time soon. I bet that the global economy will stay weak for years , and that made me Citibank's most profitable trader. And that is how I became a millionaire, because I knew the difference between the economy down here and the economy over there.

CHAPTER 4: CAREER

Gary Stevenson became an interest rate trader after he won a trading-based "card-game" in 2008 at the age of 21.

Using the 2007–2008 financial crisis to his advantage, he made less than £400,000 in his first year and by 2010, his first million.

He placed a wager on the 2011 Greek government debt crisis. By the end of 2011, Stevenson had estapublished himself as "Citibank's most profitable trader" by capitalizing on his belief that the wealthy tended to save their money rather than spend it, instead putting it into Real Estate and that this would prevent interest rates from rising as a result of the impact of wealth inequality on demand because wealthy people preferred to save their money and invest in in Real Estate rather than squander it.

In 2014, Stevenson then 27 years old, decided to quit trading and enrolled in the University of Oxford to pursue an economics degree. "Depressed and disillusioned," feeling that "change isn't going to come from there," and frustrated with the education he was getting, He engaged with the writings of Ludwig Strain, At of Mian and Amir Sufi, Emmanuel Saez, Gabriel Zucman, and Thomas Piketty.

When the COVID-19 pandemic started, he predicted there would be a rise in house prices and retail costs.

He founded the YouTube channel GarysEconomics with the goal of educating the general public about economics and joined the Patriotic Millionaires to advocate for a wealth tax.

Along with 29 other Uk millionaires, he sent an open letter to Rishi SunK In 2021, urging the prime minister to implement a wealth tax and stating that

"Instead of raising national insurance and taking £1,000 a year away from families on universal credit, the chancellor, who is a multimillionaire, should be taxing himself and people like me —people with wealth.

Additionally, he also suggested restricting the amount of time that people can keep their wealth.

Stevenson made an appearance in the

Channel 4 program Has the Bubble Burst in Cryptocurrency? in 2022.

His autobiography, The Trading Game, was purchased by Penguin Books for a six-figure sum.

Gary Stevenson - Life Out of Balance, a short film directed by Stefan Roe Griffiths, included Stevenson in 2023.

CHAPTER 5: TRADING JOURNEY

"By betting inequality was going to destroy our economy and make the poorest in society even poorer," Gary Stevenson amassed a multimillionaire fortune.

He attained his aim by the age of 22, gaining a position as a trader at Citigroup in Canary Wharf in 2008. He made his first million in two years. His bets that interest rates wouldn't rise and the gap between the rich and the poor would widen made tens of millions of dollars for the bank, and his compensation and bonuses kept going up.

Then he quit. ***"I was making more money than I could ever imagine,"*** Stevenson says from his flat in Limehouse, overlooking the Citi tower he formerly worked in. However, it wasn't correct.

"You know how I made the money? I bet on what is a fucking disaster," he continued.

"I'm betting on the world economy collapsing over time. No joke at all, right? You know, that's going to kill people. Families will suffer irreversibly, and things will only grow worse. Take a look at the current state of affairs with the cost of living crisis. Half of this

country will not have enough money to turn on the heating in the winter".

Stevenson didn't, however, just quit his previous position. Now, he is fighting the system he was employed by, running campaigns to educate the public about the unfair things that bankers such as himself are doing in the glittering towers of Canary Wharf and the City of London in order to "continue to make the economy unfair."

As we go along the Thames from his apartment to his former Canary Wharf office, he said **"The only way to change the system is to make the people really fucking angry about** *it." "You know, I used to make a million pounds a year working in that building there. Now I'm out here giving away information for free, and it's not like the media is all over me — the establishment doesn't want the people to know the truth."*

CHAPTER 6: GARY'S TRADING TRICKS

In one of Gary's Videos he talked about the secret to wealth and how the Rich keep getting even more richer.

"When I was a kid, all the money my family made was from my dad's job. Now, most ordinary families are like this, when they think about money, when they think about wealth. It's not about work and a job, but from working in the city, I realized that for very rich families, things are different. For them, it's not about work, it's about wealth. Now wealth is not about what job you do, or how hard you work, wealth is about what you do own.

Now, I think for most of us, it's so hard just to get a house that we don't really realize how much work there is in society. It's not just about houses and flats and I live here in Canary Wharf, all of those big skyscrapers in wharf, all those big skyscrapers in the city they are owned as well, and it's not just the skyscrapers, right? Walk down the street, the shopping centers, the banks, the restaurants everything is owned. You might be thinking. I don't know anyone who owns a skyscraper. I don't know anyone who owns a shopping center. The reason for that is, unlike houses that ordinary people own, all of this commercial wealth, commercial property, the vast majority is owned by the richest individuals and families in our society. So the point is, there is a huge amount of wealth that exists in the world and I want you to think about this next time you walk down the street. Look at all the shops, look at all the restaurants, all the bars, all the pubs, and think to yourself, somebody owns this.

All of the wealth that exists is owned. But it goes deeper than that because there are a lot of things that ordinary people do own. Ordinary people do own their own house or the flat that they live in. A lot of the time the only way they can do that is through debt. Now, debt is like negative wealth if you buy a flat for €£200,000 you only really own 25% of that flat. Now that loan doesn't come from nowhere. It comes from the bank and ultimately comes from the wealthy individuals who own that bank. So what that means is even the things we do own like our houses, often even those things are indirectly owned by the wealthiest people in our country via the debt that we have to take to buy them.

This is true for the government as well. Now when we're talking about the physical world that exists in our cities and our country, there are all things that are owned by the government; the schools, the hospitals, police stations, and fire stations, but if we look at the data gathered by French economics Thomas, Piketty, he estimates that the government debt is worth more than all of the wealth: all of the schools, and the hospitals are owned by the government. What that means is that the wealthy people also own all of the schools and hospitals in this country. But it actually goes deeper than that because it's not just that the richest people own all of the wealth in our society, they actually make a huge amount of money just from owning them and that money doesn't come out of nowhere. It comes from people like you and me. Now the most obvious example of that is if you rent a house or rent a flat— you work here in London—probably at the end of the month, a third of your pay goes straight to paying the rent and that goes to the owner of the house. If you own your own property the same thing is going to happen with your mortgage.

Now that money doesn't disappear, that money goes from you to the person who owns the property or the mortgage which in most cases will be a wealthy person. But this isn't just a case of property. This happens every single time you spend money. When you pay your bills that money is going towards the owners of the energy and gas companies and the owners of those natural resources. When you go to the supermarket to buy groceries , that money doesn't all go to the workers in a supermarket, a big chunk of it goes towards the owner of the supermarket and the Owner of the building. Every single time you spend money, every single time you make money, a big chunk of that money is going from you to the owners of the wealth. It's easy for us not to think about this kind of money that comes from only wealth, because for most of us we get our money from working a job, but the richest people they get most of their money from this wealth income, income that comes from the things that they own and the size of it can be enormous.

Someone who has a wealth of 2 million pounds can make an income of about 60,000 pounds every year just from the wealth that they own and that is enough to live a pretty good life. But very wealthy individuals, they can make a lot more. Someone who has a wealth of 10 million pounds, they'll probably make 300, 000 pounds every single year just for the things that they own.

If we look at Jeff Bezos who has an estimated wealth of 200 billion Dollars, this guy if he makes just a 3% return on his wealth he's gonna make 6 billion Dollars every single year.

What you need to realize is that whilst we are out here working for our money these super rich people, they're making tens, hundreds, even billions of pounds or dollars every single year without working at all. Just from the money they earned from this wealth. It's important to realize, like I have said, that money is not coming from nowhere, that money is coming from the money that you and I spend.

Recently the wealth of the richest people in our society not just the top 1% but the top 0.1% or 0.01%, has exploded. These guys get a massive amount of income every year from their wealth. all the money they make over the course of their life.

Imagine you're Jeff Bezos and he's making every single year 6 billion Dollars which is about 20 million Dollars a day or something, he can't spend all of that money, this tells you something important about the difference between ordinary people and the super-rich.

Ordinary people spend the money they make whereas the super-rich save the money they make.

In a strong economy that's not necessarily a bad thing, they can save that money, and invest it into growing businesses, and the economy can grow but when we have a weak economy, like what we've had definitely since 2008 the companies don't wanna invest and they don't wanna grow so it creates a problem right? These super-rich guys are making huge amounts of money every year from their wealth and they can't invest it, so what are they gonna do? Well if they can't invest it, there is one other thing they can do. They can buy your mum's house! That is what happens in a weak economy that is very unequal, the rich own all of the wealth, which means they generate a massive amount of cash flow from the rest of us every single year, but they can't invest it because the economy isn't growing. So instead they use that money to buy wealth from the rest of us to buy our houses for example and that is why you're seeing my generation (younger people) are unable to get houses when our parent's generation was able to get them because we are gonna have to compete with the huge amounts of income from the super rich who wanna buy the houses as well, that's why we've seen houses in this country go up from 2-3 times the average wage to 20-30 time.

If the rich are getting more and more income and they're using it to buy our wealth well that means next year the rich are gonna get even more income from us which they're gonna use to buy even more of our wealth.

When I say wealth, I'm talking about things that we need like houses we need to raise our families in. It's very important to understand income is about work whereas wealth is about ownership of things. This ownership is super super unequal. The rich own almost all of the wealth in society which means a huge amount of money gets transferred from ordinary working people to the rich every year they use that money to buy the stuff that makes us poorer. The cycle is gonna get worse and worse and worse unless we do something about it, so what do we have to do?

The big problem here is that the money that you and I make from working gets taxed differently from the money that the super-rich make from their wealth. Our money when we work gets taxed at source and we have to pay that tax but rich people get their money in different ways: capital gains, inheritances, trusts, these methods of getting income is much much easier to avoid taxes. If we allow that to happen it is inevitable that more and more wealth is gonna get transferred from workers to these super rich families that is gonna mean that ordinary workers in the future are not gonna be able to afford houses.

Unless we do something about this inequality, unless we make sure the super-rich at least pay the same rate of tax that the rest of us pay, nothing's going to change, that is our future's gonna be a space where all of our money goes on just paying for the basics of life, and we can never own houses and the super-rich own houses what that means is if you were born poor you will die poor and if you were born rich you will die richer.

For me(Gary Stevenson), that's not the kind of future I wanna live in.

My ultimate message is we need to find a way to make sure the super richest start contributing back to society, especially through tax.

CHAPTER 7: CONCLUSION

Gary Stevenson gave up his trading profession because he believed that the only way to improve the global economy was to address inequality. Since then, he has worked with economic think tanks, studied for an MPhil at Oxford, and started the YouTube channel GarysEconomics, where he teaches people about economics in everyday situations.

In addition to writing for publications like OpenDemocracy and the Guardian, he frequently appears on radio and television.

Printed in Great Britain
by Amazon